Eternity's Beautiful Edge

Genesis Burkley

BookLeaf Publishing

Presentation by *BookLeaf Publishing*

Web: www.bookleafpub.com

E-mail: info@bookleafpub.com

ISBN: 9789357446273

First edition 2023

This book is dedicated to everyone who ever came into my life, be it for a short time or is still here, and held my hand through this wild journey. You, more than anyone, hold the keys to the various doors I'm about to lay open for all to see. Guide others through, that they may see themselves like you helped me see myself. And for anyone who doesn't believe they are ready for such an adventure, ask yourself this: what if?

ACKNOWLEDGEMENT

To my best friend, who knows my every thought, every deed, every action and every desire, and still sees me through a lens of pure love. Thank you for listening to me, and not just listening, but truly hearing me, in the moments I felt everything from heard. Thank you for never doubting me. For always emboldening me, renewing strength within me. Thank you for sharing my pain with me, when no one else was there, or when I believed no one else cared enough to be there, you were there. This is truly, for You.

To my mother, Gail, look ma, we made it! All those years you told me these words would touch another soul, here they go. May they travel on the wings of your prayers each night and May the eyes and hearts that need them most, be loved and seen through them. This is for You.

To my father, Skip, I may not have gone down the path you wanted for me, but you taught me how to be nothing less than authentically me. And I want you to know, this is me. A side of me you may have never seen before but a more real part of me nonetheless. I pray it not only makes you proud but helps you see yourself in me. This is for You.

To my older brothers, Joshua, Ric, and Jeffrey, thank you all, for all the years of laughter and support, especially through my illness. You helped raise your little brother, whether it was beating me in video games, teaching me everyday life skills like how to hang a television on a wall, or how to use your passion as a means to heal others, you all have given me so much to be thankful for as your little brother. This one's for You!

To my sister, Crystal, still, besides mom, the most beautiful woman on Gods green, thank you for caring for me even in secret. And thank you for allowing me the privilege and opportunity to be a part of your sons life. You both will always share a special place in my heart from now and throughout eternity. This one's for You!

To my brothers in arms, Jordan, Brian, James, Eric, Cordell, Jaye, Miah, Scott, Marc, TJ, Samuel, Chris, Daniel, and many more, my sisters in arms, Sierra, Samantha, Erin, Amy, Maghen, Danielle, Rachel, and many more, to my musical mentors, Marshall, Aaron, Michal T, Michael J, this one's for all of You!

To my grandmother, Nana, thank you for all the delicious oatmeal early in the mornings before school, all the times you would change the channel from Wheel of Fortune to Power Rangers for me, the many many nuggets of wisdom, and for forever watching over me especially when I've been closer to you than ever. This one's for You!

To anyone I may have forgotten, you're not forgotten. Let this book show you how seen you really are. Let's open a door together. A door to forever. Thank you.

PREFACE

When I was a little boy, I had this notebook. It was supposed to be used for taking science notes. With every page of scientific research, there was a poem, a song, lyrics that served as a reference for the notes. What became a simple pastime, turned into a habit, an addiction. The words would never stop. Around age 9, I heard my first rap song, sitting in the garage with my dad as he polished his ‘67 Camaro SS. That’s when I decided to put voice to those feverishly loud words spilling onto every page. Now, some almost 30 years later, barely scratching the surface of my life, I have yet to even begin to share with the world, my love for wordplay. Let this be a love letter, to anyone or anything who ever inspired me to put thoughts to pages: You, the reader are my ultimate inspiration, and I pray this would inspire you as well.

A Drink from the Deep
Vol.MCCXMMMCCCXVI

Sometimes you need love
Without it you have no life
Drink from the deep often

Found inside the gem
Born from fire, forged in steel
A light in the depths

Worlds apart in time
Looking up to the same star
Drinking from the deep

October 1st, 2017

Walking the perimeter, fidgeting with twitter feeds, in the mood for dancing some gambling and some Krispy Kreme. Seen a few Missy's that wanna drink and smoke and nix these jeans, Aldean, hundreds of fans out, save 53. Turn the corner, I saw the strip and both hotels, known well where I stay, but maybe I'm just grown swell. Text just hit my phone, cell tone more like no mail, it read,"I miss you and I hope you're having fun, get home well." I look up and saw a window busted near the middle floor, second one burst open like a random shock that hit the floor. What's in store next I couldn't have guessed but it's in store, 33 Guns and bullet laden shells ready to rip thru cores. Shots fired and yes I immediately hit the ground, Music died, all that's left is silence and the pistol sounds. Rifle artillery wish I had a sniper scope here with me I would try to drop whoever devised this killing plot quickly. Instantly more shots rang out, I see the patrons ducking and diving, all the while

My phone is trying to tell me what the hell is happening. I swipe up and saw a text from Gabbie that read,"I'm watching live are you alive or you dead?!" She said,"Answer me please!" I replied with a pic of myself behind a brick wall, sweating saying I'll call in a sec. I dialed cops then hung up. I called her back like "you good?" She's started crying saying please stay alive, I said that I would. I was like stay on the line. I hopped up and made a B Line to the nearest wall complex so I could think and reminded back to our first kiss in her apartment, at the start it was the smartest, she was single young and flawless I was older, some accomplice, held and harnessed love regardless for this goddess I would honestly be astonished if I didn't make it back to LA. But now that time is ours I thought I'd show her just in case it's over, took the ring out of my pocket, snapped a pic and said,"it's yours if I make it home from this. Wait by your phone for a bit." I hung up and proceeded to find the floor he's on real quick. Looking like I stayed there hit the elevator like,"I don't have a gun on me, how am I gone make this right?" Looked up then I saw a shadow in the ceiling by the light, saw it was a glock 40, took it out and cocked it right. One in the chamber, several in the magazine, took that last pic happily and said,"I love you Gabbie, please remember me if I don't make it out of this alive, either this is right or my fatal attempt to try. It was this, marry you, or maybe one day suicide, or at least with truth inside I could say i subdued my pride and proved that I am just as capable as I never knew, blessings true, I'll see you again honey, Peace." The line cut and I shut all the lights out, heard the rifle fire from the room that I must find now. Saw the door wide open, I guess they thought to fight now, so I crept forward acting like everything's alright now. Waited for my eyes to adjust to the darkness, sat and breathed regardless of fear trying to spark this, I took a deep breath, and open fire at the target. One shot two shot three shots he'd fallen. Leg shot chest shot chest shot I'm stalling, ran in and stood over his body like I'm on this. Kicked the gun away so he couldn't respond then looked in the room for anyone else that was going to do him harm. No one was there I came back and he was still breathing, he said,"I didn't mean it, I truly just believe that our world is going to hell, North Korea bout to strike back, I had to show the world that this is how we fight back. Guerrilla warfare, no fair they take our knights and run them into the ground like PTSD and Iraq. That's when I said,"well unlike you, I stand up for rights Jack. No one could protect themselves, you think that's how our lives match? I promise you it won't be trump or Kim Jung Un that lights that shot heard round the world when the missiles hit our ice caps. It'll be a nice black hole where there was life at, you wanna end this yourself or let me end you before your nights black?" He said,"take me out but enjoy the time you have left." I showed him a picture of Gabbie that made his hands sweat. He said she's beautiful, then I showed him the ring. He said please marry her if for no one else then for me. I believe with a mind like yours, you can change the world. Take the hand of that little girl and let your truth unfurl." Last click in the chamber hit his forehead, no more dead. I called her up and said,"it's over, I'm coming home kid. I took the mag out the gun and fired the last shot. First stop for me ended up being my last stop. Put it on the ground got in the elevator, went down, and saw the land locked. Found the nearest officer and led him to the scene, told him the story and he put me in cuffs till we convened. A day later I was praised as a hero. Made it home to Gabbie, at the terminal so many people cheered tho. She pushed her way through the crowd, our picture taken loud. One kiss, One bullet what's the difference in the Sound? For Stephen Paddock, the only difference is silence, for The onlookers of violence, the difference is time spent. For me, i just found that this moment is all we have, she asked about it later I said this is the choice I had. Let him bleed out or have a conversation and then end his pain, so deranged

only open to me cuz I closed in range. Hopeless stain painted on my life like a black spoken page the source of rage within me has dissipated to Hope and Grace. Gabrielle I want to let you know that you are not alone, I could be a hero today but nothing changes why I'm
Home. To be with you to hold you tight to show you love is all I know, in the wake of tragedy let's dream a dream that's all our own.

Do 4 Luv (Excerpt)

Just when I thought my heart was buried
Locked away and the key left dead in the cemetery
It wasn't scary I just really couldn't carry
All these feelings and emotions that tarry
They leave me daring to exercise all my rights to end myself when all the stress gets hairy
I've been searching my life for a magic fairy
Someone who could shift the whole game away from something so dreary
I keep on staring at the clock
Hoping barely for the merriest of merry thoughts to penetrate me there and I see
The beauty in your eyes no one is comparing
I'm leery but more like Larry to run away on contrary
Baby you fly as a canary
Someone spare me from this wariness unfairly laid upon me like that girl named Carrie
I'm way to Indy to be Jackson like I'm Gary
But rarely have I felt this type of love sometimes it gets utilitary
And even if my heart gets buried by this chariot
I'm praying for this little girl you hear me?
I'm a sucker for love

Inheritance

They always told me I would never do it
Young black and gifted in the prison system, that's my future
So many family members saying so long and I never knew you
Until I become a billionaire, now they all pursue me
But it's my duty to my community
If I'm truly king then my fiefdom gotta be taken care of, this ain't like in the movies
But if I'm truly a king then isn't my duty to my queen
Or are those just more gender roles that we try to keep refuting?
I'll make this brief cuz my soap box is week
I'll be here all month
My years been looking bleak
My destiny is not segregated to speak
If God gave me hands and feet
Then I'll kick up dust as I preach
And if you need a sign let me remind you
I was never designed to live a life primed to
Signal the time to rise and give hell to who tries to

Feed you these lies that keep you dying to cry too
Our neighborhoods have drive bys when the sky's blue
Demons arrive to seed in you kilos and crime moves
So when you seek to see Jesus inside you do things that you'd like to see
Remember satan is keen to disguise too
Eyes of an eagle from the highest of heights
We dive from the sky and pierce the darkness with light
That's why the lamp is brightest at night
Gotta be awake for whenever something rolls around the corner looking for fights
This is war time
I mean pick up your sword time
Scholars pick up a pen and get ready for lord lines
Cuz the more I'm given this gift the more that I share it
If I'm young black and beautiful
Then where's what I inherit?

Real Lyfe

Waiting for the promise to fulfill from the seed
We planted the grass in the garden of Eve
We watched the trees grow this was more than a dream
Now I've seen what it means to see the cost of belief
Eden was bread from heaven this illogical feast
Garnered the peace most dodge cuz they honored deceit
Pardon the weak but hold down the strongman in your speech
Atlas held up the world drowning and was brought to his knees
Thoughts of needs this is but a stalk in the weeds
Puff on your trees now but it's for naught when you breathe
Flowers erode away and air gets tossed in the seas
That's why there's so much life lost when you cough and you bleed
It's more than pain more than pleasure
More than fame more than heaven
More disdain so disheveled
Sowed in rain sort the pebbles
Pour in drains sordid mental

For the game on my level
I'm ashamed but I'll get better
Sign my name that's my tether
In this life I got two goals
Build a legacy that can set my family up 2 fold
Then show the world that a little boy from
Illinois was ill and annoyed and just got too bold
Put the scriptures to work before he got too old...

My Last Verse

I couldn't pick a better more perfect time
To get at you in the spirit and spit a line
Girl this a hidden vine a three stranded chord that was wrote for us
Coursing thru my veins is this potent stuff
You open up my mind to a beautiful vision
I used to see me inside a beautiful prison
And you on the other side
Walking away with each day and time
Many years spent in solace thinking how can i describe
You're married now I know you were such a beautiful bride
Probably pregnant now
Graduated college and in your stride
Life's kinda scary now but I promise what a wonderful ride
I let you go deep inside but your hand I still do admire
If I'm honest, I'm looking for a girl just like you
Who writes songs and sings the books just like you
Who ignites things deep in my mind that aren't spiteful
Who whenever I think about makes me feel like

Michael
I'm at home
And now I'm on a throne
As much as you might be gone you're sitting right next to me
Blessing me
Most call this obsession I call this lyrical heavenry
No more of this verbal weaponry
Really wish you'd message me
Even just to tell me whatever it is you're telling me
Redeeming Dance of this Story I love you endlessly
And in my dying day I hope that they read this and you feel blessed to be
A part of my story and the reason I died in peace
I'm a few years from the grave but still that close to His feet
And when it's He that I meet ima ask Him to save you
I know you know His voice but I think me and you were faded into nothingness
Too brave to face what was coming miss
You focused on goals and I focused on doubling it
I was out my government
My element was covered in blood

I moved back home and ended up almost flubbing it
You know why I'm scared? Cuz I've got no legacy
Nothing to show for all the years I've given endlessly
But I have one thing and you'll remember me well
That one boy that taught you love was more than anything frail
It was brave it was fearless and it never said no
No matter what happened to it it was everything gold
So bambina I hope you have a happy birthday
Jan 19, Mar 16, that's 3 months and 3 days...

Missin U, In Tears Verse

I'm loving your light
Vulnerable
I'm up every night
Calling you home
Knowing God has a plan
Even if I don't see
That's what Faith is to Love
Hope to believe
See you the flower that I gotta protect
You the child that I gotta respect
You every single cloud in the sky opened up to the sun
And I love the way your heart is opened up to the Son
Son of a gun
Master of the Army of Heaven
Arming my brethren just in case we gotta war in the nexus
Sword in my center
That's what loving you feels like but it's better
Than calling a hooker and losing all my bread and my cheddar
See I wanna be here wit you
Fighting fears wit you
Every tear wit you like a clear issue

I wanna bottle it up and hold In time till I'm 80
Then show the ocean when you gone it can't let go of my baby
I wanna hold you hair back when you throwing up with our baby
And if you want some Doritos and peanut butter that's crazy
But I'll never be lazy
Treat you like the queen that you are
From here to the nearest star girl you're more real than my heart
See you the rib that was taken from me when I was sleeping
I remember every girl I messed wit when I was creepin
I remember every time I didn't wait for you
Threw some hate on you
For not being in my life to save me for you
I remember almost committing suicide on the low
Not even thinking bout how that would change your whole life growth
How we never would've met
Never would've got the chance to say yes at the altar
All because I done faltered
I remember the first day that we met
Them golden shoes told me you walk the path in heaven that was set

And singing praises up to heaven had me
Knowing you're blessed
So don't even stress love
I'll keep praying till you're home in my vest

Who She Is Pt 1

She was a child
Growing up in a beautiful house
Off the coast at the summit of a mountain
She was smart
Sunrises and sunsets set her apart from the stress of being oppressed and torn apart by life
She was a smile
That radiated the light from the Son like the heat vision from the eyes of Superman she was a Superfan of all things truth
She was a laugh
That infected everybody, worse than Covid she was the coat when it's cold out to your frozen body
She was Peace
When you need a moment to breathe
And moment to sneeze or just a moment to believe
She was Faith
When the Son needed a mother
To teach and walk by that and not by sight
Until the moment He was brought under...

Little Heart O'Mine

Ashamed to spit
Anxious from everything I did
Dangerous
Doctors coming in and out pacing as if
I'm not laying right here doc say something!
Lemme know if it's all bad
Lemme know if I should call dad
He knows that if I'm gone in the next 20
minutes he won't know how to be a grown man
Lemme see my mom and just tell her I'm sorry
for being the son that she lost bad
When I should've been praying in a monastery
with no monetary I was chasing ass
Now I face the facts
That at any moment I could zone in and out like
a sonic stage
Rip my heart out with all my rage
And figure it all out before I age
This is worse than I had imagined
Can they save me or is it past it?
I never had a baby or became a dad
And I know I'm crazy but I wish I had
Still Aladdin
Dreaming of a princess with an interest in quick
fast rapping

And chick so bad she could kick your ass
Does kick ass fashion and has different passions
Maybe she became a doctor too
Saw my chart and didn't know what a doc should do
But instead of crying she took a sigh in and didn't deny that we might not make it thru
But said she would do her best
Or find the best that would do their best
Told me just to rest
And remember this
And just feel my chest
This is my test
God what's happening
I know I didn't deserve this for the life I lived
Cuz if I did and you're fair as shit
Then alotta people should die in the place I'm in
But if not and this is my spot and shit just got hot
And life's on the block
And I'm not in shock or dying from rot
Then please take my heart and keep it on lock
I believe more than I've ever received when I stop
So before you put me lost in a box
Make this seed produce crops…

Something Woke Up

this is a heaven sent message
Delivered distances delicate
To remind you of the Bible's parenthetical and prophetical epithets
Weapons that have been set against men
Ready to stretch our flesh
Hence the beast of the hoard is ready to shake us to death like an etch-a-sketch
Records that tells us that in the end when men have taken a beating half to death
Been defeated and left for dead with breath reeling
One man will split the sky revealing for all time
That God is not only alive and well but a man ready to get recompense
See He was wrongfully beaten broke and bent
Crucified Jesus Christ is the Maker of all that's left
And in flesh He will undo what was done in less than a sec
He will break open the clouds and announce what must commence
He will speak to the face of Death and decree in dreadful depth

That the deeds that Death had dealt won't
deceive those diligent
But instead the feast that's meant for the hoards
of evil guests will start with heads of state and
those ones who kill our best
They will be brought before the Throne of
Mercy and Judgment and the Judge will render a
verdict to bleed them where they slept
Now believe this when I mention
that Peace for which we've wept
We will see it with each head that careens down
evil steps

Who Is She Pt 2

She is Grace
Her words like a tapestry of beauty
Sometimes moody but who isn’t when this is your duty?
She is Power
I mean strength greater than Hulk
You can’t see that punch to the gut coming but you know when it hits
She is Joy
Not just a joke or a witty punchline
She’s that one time after one time that keeps you going when you don’t want time
She is Kind
The kinda kind that makes up its mind to do things that would make your spine tingle cuz you know it’s right
She is Hope
When the Light left this world and the sky darkened and we hid in a cave not knowing what next, she held on, she was strong, she was shelter from that storm, she helped everyone know that truth was shed on that day and it’ll come back home...

The Victim

Satan the victim
Hate is within him
Maybe it's vision
Or maybe he been blind to derision
Foresight was off when he twisted
All the angels that sought to get with him
I promise God don't like ugly but forgiveness was written
When Jesus took a stroll up the hill
Holding a plank of wood
Thank the Good Lord with His sword that He saved us through it
The fate of the good and the guilt of the lonely
Man he so mad because he felt stabbed in the back by his homie
But his homie had given rules to the highest of all
He denied it for all
Eternity
The highest would fall
Crying and all
Trying to deny what he saw
Like God you traitor
Ima take and make all your giants as small
As an ant

Deep in their sin they'll be dying and all
Hope will be lost
That's why I'm in disguise when I call
I look good huh?
Still got my beauty
Cuz they can't see close enough or even get that close to me
I made their life such a movie
Some seek fame and some seek the power
Others seek riches and to attain it
Their forgiveness was ours
I would never plead the 5th
Jesus a fake and a coward
Have Him stand up at the podium and speak this hour
Say you God cuz all I see is a snake in the flower
Painted white but when cooked up
Be in them veins like the powder
Clogging them up
Your saints were supposed to be ordained with this power
To raise dead bodies and heal sickness
I ain't seen it I'm proud of the fact that
Anytime my demons move
Change is devoured
We make slaves every hour
To pornographic pages and sour
Notes that been tainted with louder

Voices like take this you coward
And after you swallow this pill you'll be wit
Satan and I'll tower
Over the children you bled for
Yes LORD I said LORD
I am the Lord of Hatred and I've made it my honor
To take your place at the gates that angels vacate when our
Army comes marching in like the saints should but nah
Homie I'm lit...

The Defender

Hush Satan I've heard enough of your anguish
You're angry I see your face
But what happens will be the case
I trust in my mighty soldiers cuz I have shown them the way
It's more than written in books
It's inscribed on their hearts with grace
And they choose it everyday
though it's hard and they fight to pray
They will not become the prey
Of your sinister ways today
My plan is set in motion
My hand is open to save
I take what you made as workers
And change their whole frame from slave
Bondservant as Paul called it
Out there paving the way
For generations to come
And it starts with the power to say
I believe in Jesus and today is my first day
To get back down on my knees
and know it's gone be ok
This is Faith
So go head satan do all of your Evil deeds
I promise you when you leave

The only hole left in me
Will be that you couldn't join us
In holy matrimony
I'd die for my faithful bride
You'd just die and that's it you see?
We been toe to toe with each other and I'm done losing my breath
You want war? Loosen them straps and go hard like you would to death
And when all of your energy spent
And all of your demons rest
The only things that you'll feel
Is that hole you put in my chest
In your chest
You ain't got flesh so you can't bleed but you will
You'll scream and cry and whine for eternity and I'll feel
So justified by my works
That I'll try and send you a meal
Matter of fact I'll eat it right in your face
and leave you the BILL
I'm ILL no I'm HEALED
I'm SKILLED no I'm SKILL
And each and every one of my soldiers are down to kill
And we will March upon your kingdom
With chains for y'all for real
with Praises to our Father

In honor of His return
With Fire I'll let it burn
I bring you my Son, the Filled
His name is Genesis
But you can call him shadow
You can't see him
Facts demon
I wish you had them eyes to see
That's decent
But you lack the teaching
In fact he's preaching
And when you fact check him
I'm sure he'll just laugh pleased that he's
Really a rap feature
He don't need a mansion car or the clothes
He'd never testify about how I gave him some
hoes
He's always been down to ride even when things
got close
But he'd never suffer the wrath
That you'll suffer forever more
This is right Musix...

Who She Is Pt 3

She will be New
I mean like stepping out of a shower
Getting your hair done nails done everything did
Not worrying about the worldview of your curls
or your curves
She will be Fire
I mean set the world ablaze
Stopping nuclear winter from happening
The type of fire that removes the plight and
renews the earth
She will be Benevolent
Taking risks for others to see their beauty
Taking each moment as it comes to her
Rising up and taking others with her
She will be Love
The kind of love that faces the storm hand in
hand
The kind of love that breaks down walls with a
gentle caress
The kind of love that, when you sit in despair in
your room, speaks one kind word and blows
away the darkness, showing you the Light you
live in is far greater than you've ever known

She is the reflection of eternity, the mirror to Love, the Promise you've hoped for. Wait. She's coming home…

God’s Blood Freestyle

Ayo they call me Genesis
First one to step in this
Last one to leave so I’ll clean up for I exit this
Get it? Exodus my whole life biblical
Rip up ya dang ritual for thinkin it was principal
Me? I keep it physical
Logical it’s critical
Every curve on point just like an elliptical
My soul spiritual had to get my bless up
Never rocked a Jesus piece cuz Jesus love is better
His Blood keeps me wetter than tsunamis in the coast
While all I brag and boast about is God don’t forget Him
I pack heat in the back seat
My Bible Lebron while my concordance D Wade if you ask me
Fact check me, our God made the universe
Coldest album to drop, and every sky is a coolest verse
Even when dudes recruit proof and lay subdued in hearse
The curse of death was broken and openly it was ruined worse

He gave us life so we could show Him the truest work
Our hearts made to love and be loved that's such a truth it hurts
Cuz most of us would rather rag on the gospel
Slam an apostle for His stance on the gospel
Matthew Mark Luke all ran with the God Son
But Thomas the only one who got a hand full of Gods blood
And still lived to tell it I won't embellish Nathan
I smell the stench and see the darkness deep in Hell is satan
And I don't hate him I hate what he does
I wish he'd change but if he changed there'd be nothing but love
And we put here to change the world
Rearrange the world
Trust the muscle that's the Spirit that's gone raise the world
He payed the world His ultimate price
He gave His life after a roll of the dice
For His clothes and His light
He let go and said no to this life
Three days later he rose like the dough that you like
And He told His holy brethren to speak boldly and fight
And though some of you may die, you'll behold me in sight and be like

"Jesus is that you? I can't believe my eyes!"
I seem alive but you died does this mean we have died?
He says yes and now it's our time to pray
And intercede for the world which is falling into decay
Depravity at it's worse when the Savior just wants our freedom from demons and we believe in the heathen so we delete em
And beat em
Keep on breathin and eating
And March on toward the mark of maturity as you see Him
You need Him, shoot I need Him
I'm wrong all the time
Spit God given lines then in the same line kick a rhyme
That has less to do with God and way more to my shine
I act sublime when I'm really just dirt and some grime
But I been cleaned up
Fresh cut coming out the box hot
Labels don't know what to do with me cuz I will not stop
You give me a stage and a mic and I will rock shop
The crowd don't know the verse or the music but they know ABBA

The Fatha! The Holy Trinity it's an honor
To present to you these words of worship in sonata
I don't need no katana or burrito or horchata
I just need my Papa and I'm out Bruh…

Prayer XVI

Chorus - There's a light within
Deep inside, there's a fight in Him
Even when the darkest night gets grim
There's a Light within

I'm calling out to you Lord
Because I need your help
If I didn't believe in You
I couldn't see myself
Be myself
Sometimes it's hard to need myself
I need thy help
And in time I'll seek thy help
Trust in only one savior
There is no other option
Such a venomous concoction
Every night, it's got me boxed in
And every night I try to stop it
But I can't seem to shake it
Break fast when the morning comes
And that's how I know I've made it
I'm sated
But sometimes I hunger for hatred
The belly of the beast grumbles often
It ain't ate yet

I need to wake up!
I'm steady sleeping the sleep of death
With every breath I speak from my chest
I'm not relieved I need my rest
When I look in the mirror I don't know who I'm staring at
Preparing my body for war
Sharing my pain to be exact
Lord Jesus!
Please hear me
Please be near me
I need the fear of the Lord
Not others to fear me
I need to see clearly
When I speak please hear me
I try to walk this road
But every step makes me weary
Help me find the strength to stay by your side
And when I can't walk
Please carry me by your side
And when it's my time
Let me be found by your side
And let the world know that in you
And for you I cried…

Untitled VI

There's beauty in the struggle
Ugliness when you confess
Like how's it truly feel to be yourself in front of guests?
Somewhat so different ain't it
Lemme paint the perfect picture portrait so you can piece the puzzle and project a powerful person plainly
I was mangey
Dreads healthy but knot
Staying up day and night yet wasn't making a-lot
Finally almost lost my life twice in the same year
Same fears I had about never making it became clear
I was looking for a love to change me
Rearrange me
I was feeling so broken and open
How could you blame me?
And when one left me colder I was swallowed by hell
I ain't too afraid to acknowledge myself and ask for help
When she left I felt crucified

Truth is I died to something major
I would never been another persons favor
Or someone after a particular flavor
I was only after God my Creator and Jesus my
Savior
Thank God they're one in the same
With Holy Spirit guiding me home, man I could
let my life go now and I'm great
There's so much I haven't lived yet
But truth is what I've lived has
Let me know that life might not be for me with
how I think…love yours

Luv Yours

You ever loved someone that way you think that God loves that person?
It's not bout what you get from them
But just what they deserve when
You ain't gotta hand to help them wit
You just pray
And everyday you say amen for them, your heart feels like it's bled for them?
You tend to them in spirit
You feel so near
Yet the miles are palpable you feel it
But you don't fear it
You wish you could say,"aye shorty, I mean tall girl, what's good? When I'm all better can I stroll thru yo hood?"
Acting all pimpin pimpin I gotchu but this is not a game nor a test
She just need the real not a guess
Member being real before your guests
This that dinner table moment where you chill or you confess
Now me? I got alot to say
Bout how for the past 4 years, every single day, I pray that you would see His face
And since that day, May 6th of '18

I’ve seen great things and still I’m so afraid you won’t say yes
And that’s your prerogative lady
I’m not trying to cuff you
I may be a little crazy
But my heart tells me I’d want to
Just get to know you daily
Maybe wife you if you want to
But if you just wanna be friends
That’s fine too cuz I trust you
How can you trust another you ain’t seen in a while?
Or how can you say you love somebody who ain’t been loved in this style?
I say I love you and I miss you like these words don’t have weight
But trust me I wouldn’t say them if I didn’t relate cuz their great
When I say I love you, that means I’ll give my life for you
Die for you
Some say that’s God in me but baby I see God in you
And He’s worthy of my whole life’s work
So when I tell you I love you trust me it hurts
Cuz I know what that means
When I say I miss you I mean I miss not being with you

Next to you to hold you hand or maybe just worship with you
Yea I would love to kiss you
Wipe away any issues
Whether or not this is true
I would so love to give you
Those chocolates I know you eyeing
This bracelet that you'd look fly In
That house wit that land I've plotted in
Wyoming think we could try it?
Some horses upon that land we can tend to and be riding
The sunsets and the sunrises we promise to always see shining
Together I think we'd write such beautiful music
But then I stop pause in anxiety comes fuming and I lose it
So babygirl, I'll be content wit just saying this here
This is the realest verse I've written all year

It Took Awhile

Ok, before I knew you, I knew You cuz I was praying for you
I've tried to write this verse 3 times so ima say this to you
It takes some courage to say what I'm bout to say
So I hope it can help you laugh, smile, cry, and even pray
I'm a whole case, a whole dictionary in your whole face
A bold face but still a shy and really cold face
To be honest, it's you're birthday and I don't know what to say
I guess a great place to start would be, how's your day?
Oh by the way, I got this present that I made
But I can't give it to you now, oh the sense it wouldn't make
Maybe later in this song you'll understand why this was made
Or how I've saved these words inside like a road that must be paved
I will say this, you know what I miss most about you?

The fact that every time you stepped into a room
I felt the Ghost about you
Not to be loopy but truly you're like a movie
And every year is an epic
I hope Marvel is still recruiting
Cuz I'd cast you as Jubilee
In every scene you'd be shooting fireworks out
your hands
Making enemies scream
Lemme get a little bit deeper out denial
I haven't swam in a long time
And Gods still working on my crooked smile

It's Really Been Awhile

Sometimes you wake up and see flaws
Then you pause open Psalms
Start telling yourself you're gone and you forget the truth of God
Other days you wake up strong
Praying hard
Knowing all along every lie you believed was a rock thrown right at your jaw
This is all in an attempt to show you how to get purified
The last thought on your mind at night shouldn't be hell from a suicide
Who am I to save the world? Just the Son of a king
He saved me so take my hand and His grace we can meet
I respect you for living life in constant service to the masses
Your class is measured by classes your holiness measured by asking
Seeking knocking and action on the days you lack the passion
Hands high or tucked in your pockets
Your worship is satisfaction
To His holiness

Boldly I proclaim to you a queen
When you sing you make angels weep and Jesus bare a ring
Wife you up for the rest of eternity here's the thing
I got the same idea by there's just one more verse in me I gotta get out of this crooked smile

Love In The Fall

They say I am a legend
Call me Bill Smith
Cut the check and maybe then you'll get your grill shift
Fried rice from the chinaman I still get
Why? That's like asking Alaskans why they still fish
Still gotta tell it to the people how they need it
So conceded with the demons
Got you bleeding for a peanut
Now you eating kinda good
But your cheddar ain't to seasoned
Call it young money
While I'm aging my Gouda y'all just Brie'n
These some lines you won't get until your old and wiser
I talk to God cuz He's the oldest of the colonizers
See he perfected and fermented earth with life
And if you take it for it's time
That's fine just know the price
This is why
I pray for the woman I call my wife
Cuz even if I leaf this earth
I'll still keep falling for her twice

Get it? Fallen like the autumn
And I was Stalin
Too many fancy words appalling
Now my drawings are all crawling
In my skin
Let's hit the park and keep it linking like these paper cuts
Cuz in the end I don't want you numb and dangerous
Famous but keep it off the grid like John Wick
I'm just tryna feed my rib
Maybe make a couple kids
This is big
I hope you know the language when you spit
Cuz these opps got eyes locked
We don't trust deep in the 6
This is 7
I keep her close to Heaven
I'm her lesson
When she stressing
She could pull up for the message or just bless it
I'm so 8 I keep a plate and knife sharper than my weapon
If you play the game then play to win
I quit playing when I was 11 that's 3
Trinity in me I breathe in life
So my wife could see the day
Sometime in 2025
This is why

I pray and spit these bars to make us free
I know the truth in you and me
His name is Christ
Who do you see?

www.ingramcontent.com/pod-product-compliance
Lightning Source LLC
Chambersburg PA
CBHW051737130826
49812CB00033B/893